Ancestral Throat

poems by

Danny Rivera

Finishing Line Press
Georgetown, Kentucky

Ancestral Throat

Copyright © 2021 by Danny Rivera
ISBN 978-1-64662-716-5 First Edition
All rights reserved under International and Pan-American Copyright Conventions. No part of this book may be reproduced in any manner whatsoever without written permission from the publisher, except in the case of brief quotations embodied in critical articles and reviews.

ACKNOWLEDGMENTS

"Ancestral Throat" and "Lamentation for Two Voices" in *Midway*
"Permanence" in *Dislocate*
"Notes for an Epilogue" in *The Lincoln Review*
"Ghazal" and "Separation" in *Moria*
"Observation" in *Epiphany*
"Learning," "A Brief History of the 21st Century," and "American Nocturne" in *Newtown Literary*
"Call Me Father, Call Me Wanting" and "Trust" in *The Strip*
"A Simpler Language" and "The Walk (Early Morning, Pereira)," in *Huizache*
"The Ballad of the Pantera Negra" in *The Laurel Review*
"The Bachelor Takes Inventory of All that He Owns, Values" in *Western Humanities Review*
"Harbinger" in *Timber*
"Dismissal & Reverence" in *Washington Square Review*
"Litany" in *Poetry in Performance*

Publisher: Leah Huete de Maines
Editor: Christen Kincaid
Cover Art: Robin McCauley
Author Photo: Danny Rivera
Cover Design: Elizabeth Maines McCleavy

Order online: www.finishinglinepress.com
also available on amazon.com

Author inquiries and mail orders:
Finishing Line Press
PO Box 1626
Georgetown, Kentucky 40324
USA

Table of Contents

Ancestral Throat 1

Permanence 2

Upon Receiving a Second Opinion 4

Requiem for the War Dead 6

Separation 8

Notes for an Epilogue 9

Lamentation for Two Voices 10

Observation 12

Ghazal 13

Learning 14

The Walk (Early Morning, Pereira) 15

Trust 17

American Nocturne 18

Call Me Father, Call Me Wanting 21

A Simpler Language 23

The Ballad of the Pantera Negra 24

The Bachelor Takes Inventory of All that He Owns, Values 26

A Brief History of the 21st Century 27

Harbinger 28

Dismissal & Reverence 30

Litany 31

To Lucía, hija de las luces

Ancestral Throat

In their native language the elders have taught me how to say, *I hear your skin darkening.* To be that animal is to make godless music with the wave of my tongue, a series of cymbals crashing in the orchestra pit. You stand on the land bridge separating the villages while sliding the edge of a blade upwards along your palm. *Oh vision, oh spirit* of the ancestral throat. A newspaper details the story of a woman with a taste for uncommon spices, who spent time among lesser beasts, rewriting Scripture in her own image. In a plaza north of the capital, a knot of snare drums rings tightly, a spilling of eighth notes, measure for slanted measure. Artillery shells form a crown around the caravan, reserve a claim for the earth and its daughters—spires of dirt and rock slurring the air. The outsiders will record in their discolored papers the ritual summoning of panthers, black pelts against the moon, of orphans wearing their corrupted teeth as amulets. The elders have also taught me how to say: *We will remember like the dust in our hands the man that you have failed to become.*

Permanence

The drawn mile of yet another infant made whole.

*

A concertina as disrupted grays carried over: *these fields are overrun with standing battalions.*

*

After temblors the disappearances, that unsettling gravity: the *curé*, an inverted suture.

*

Dusk clicks with the threshing of migratory thieves, unwavering, dismantling chapters.

*

Daughter. I have waited for your return all these years. What indescribable pain. Daughter.

*

The capital morning's echo, an unchartered song, in the closing of doors.

*

We will sleep on the ground, so as to be closer to our grandmother and her toys, the willow tree with its distended crown.

*

A clearing of discharged arias, *you are mine no matter the hour,* the point at which the heart screams *enough.*

*

El último descanso que me trae su voz es lo que no me aguardo negar.

*

A lace bodice unraveling after the flood, to speak of a thirst that catapults over the blues: *this tumult is all I have come to know of Heaven.*

Upon Receiving a Second Opinion

I

Your cells are dispersing and may no longer be identified.

First, tighten the fist: clear openings with her grief. *Don't be embarrassed.* Absorb the circled light above you. Withdraw veils, loosen strings from the winding childhood, and answer that pummeling. *Feel no shame.* Write a letter awakened by its own history. Translate the common song of our days into need.

I see this agony, the hour of plagues, every day.

*

In waiting rooms
for punctures,

an order to seize
the sun's

reddening peril.

*

The bed (spare as marrow, it crushes grams
        and last reaches to the womb)

is the chosen site for anointing:

sign another cross on this forehead,
        center without faith: *sin fe no hay salvación*

(rush of oil, scream of ash).

Layer all thread like ringed years,
        and encircle the wrist in worded echoes
with this baptism to recover:

What will be left of you to pronounce?

II

Memory is a note etched
into the skin,

an offering repeated
into cupped

hands.

III

                                      [tubes and pressure]

Words loosen themselves
from meaning.

IV

                                        b l a c k o u t

Antiseptics, serrated steel,
compression:

your skin opens
like a leaf on wet pavement.

Requiem for the War Dead

> *We need not know the details of history to recognize its children.*
> —Tony Tost

I
The force of light, how sharply it descends
    at this longitude
        and on what was the eighty-sixth floor

            —then the line went dead—

    is the longest contrail between cities made of glass
    and 181,436 tons of metric steel;

    is the incalculable difference between   *how do we live now,*
    and *how did we ever learn to survive?*

II
Observe that there are no questions
    except those which deserve   to remain unanswered:

    What animals are birthed from this history,
    the spaces in which we reel from explosions,

escape our names, the outlines of our figures?

    Correction: What words will future civilizations
    have to describe calamity, the steady ashen stream

settling over Murray Street? What words will translate
    to *there was a burning sensation in my mouth,*

        twin-plumes arching northward over the East River–

III
These are the years, memory, speaking to none,
after the initial bombing: sorties over Tikrit,

    a cavalcade of heavy metal, *collateral damage* at the wedding:
        shells collapse onto white linens, a caravan of dust.

Even children hold no currency here.

IV
In the late afternoon sun   crossing the 59th Street Bridge
    pilgrims in the thousands   in the air, the static of their mouths:

but where is your God?

V
Let us measure casualties not with numbers,
but with a humid presence larger

than mothers

Separation

Through the unrepentant fog of the countryside you carried
your mother's water, tore the branch from the *palo santo,*

became a man under the sun. Animals offered no comfort
in their voices, no respite from the wind. You once pulled

the offering of *maracuyá* from the ancestral vine, tasted
its course into the throat. Tying a length of rope around

the goat's hind quarters before the communal sacrifice,
you heard children praying towards the sky. The men,

accustomed to so much thirst, scored their names onto
the ground. Later, you extended the maps, followed a path

along the riverbed, held teeth and lengths of hair, rosary
beads and leaves, like relics in a shadowbox. How am I

to measure this cruelty when it is left unattended, to accept
that I am still your son, but not the last to be written in ashes?

Notes for an Epilogue
for J.M.R., in memoriam

It came for you as urgently as an invading army, a black cross on the terrain, wave after punishing wave of mortar shells and tripwire manifested

as spent vials and gauze, syringes and catheter lines: this is the shame of the man who foresees his own end, of penitence in waiting rooms,

of hospital gowns, sheared. It came for your cells, a disquiet in the marrow. Thinner like glassine the hands became, and lighter across the borrowed bed,

as you held her, *hija de las luces,* between inner elbow and wrist. The pressurized cavity rises, then fails to rise. This is the language we have learned to speak,

sotto voce, in rear pews. Your body, prepared for final display, is a vestment, unwound thread by thread. It came while you knelt at the altar, a forced call

to prayer, as bells and tones that once rang in the eardrum, caught in the throat against your will, framing a hunger that clattered across the bones.

During evening Mass, vapor rises from the censer. *Hosanna, blessed is he* whose name is no longer spoken—whose suffering is not wasted.

Lamentation for Two Voices

On the second floor of the white-brick
building they repeat your name,

> *We appreciate the concern expressed in your message,*
> *but we have exhausted all available options.*

one among hundreds, like the rogue
cells multiplying in your blood,

> *We regret to inform that no further interventions*
> *are available at this time.*

until you answer *presente*, I am here,
I am *still* here, and you rise with care

> *Please note that we are not responsible for patients'*
> *personal effects. Be aware of your surroundings.*

if not speed, each limb refusing
to move in natural sequence,

> *Press 1 for English. Oprime dos para Español. Please hold*
> *to be connected to our next available representative.*

as if seized by an explosive's blast
radius: logic and form, displaced.

> *The subject's prognosis will be updated in the medical*
> *record at our earliest convenience. Continue to hold.*

How do we respond to the body's
repeated failure to answer for itself?

> *Failure to follow the recommended dosage may result in organ damage or system shutdown.*

No matter. *Nearer to thee* is our newest
refrain, which rings like an unanswered

> *While survival rates have improved over the previous decade, the disease is largely considered incurable.*

promissory note or a blurred silhouette
against the bedroom wall, some failure

> *All safety protocols must be followed. Proceed to the nearest exit in the event of an emergency.*

of memory. And yet you persist, straining
to conjure a new language between us,

> *Have you prepared a last will and testament?*
> *Have you completed the Advance Directive?*

the simplest of men: I promise to learn
every square inch of our divide.

Observation

The choir has been dismissed,
but I am made aware

your mouth is a flare shot
at dusk that explodes in color.

Ghazal

Let us remember what was once considered impossible: they told us to shut our mouths because we were simply orphans crossing the desert.

Lying under a government-issued blanket, I dreamt that your breathing reverberated like small-arms fire, or a series of flares crossing the desert.

There are no echoes here, only the words *praise music* and *crave*, because language neglects its own shape and majesty when crossing the desert.

Against the wall we recreate our silhouettes with cloth and string, form the effigies that will replace us: mirror images of pilgrims crossing the desert.

Leading a trail ahead of the uniformed men, you briefly smelled of the earth, the leaf of your wet skin was a warning to others against crossing the desert.

To keep your memory alive, I mimic the song of the wind across our faces by running headlong toward the gates, as if a brush wolf crossing the desert.

You christened me Daniel—*he who is judged by God*—but will your Savior question or smite me—strafe the earth, extinguish His own son crossing the desert?

Learning

As a child, I looked for a wife among *los árboles grises* behind my grandfather's house, only to come across wild dogs as raw as field hands gripping the handles of their machetes,

or like the uncut sugar served with coffee *al desayuno*. In a fevered state I found her, a kneeling *mujer* in the foothills, amid spent shell casings, and a scattered growth of leaves

from *guanábana* trees: calamity of scorched earth. With a crown of condors above, I mouthed her name into the waiting air as a psalm but was split open like boars offered as gifts

to shamans waiting by the banks of the river; such were the winds, *such were the torqued winds that morning* which carried out a ministry not of faith or of spirits, but of presence

and blood, of nerve and powdered bone; into this gulf and the scent of dirt, rising, she came to greet me, memory's cavalry behind her in a wave that would frighten and thrash

even the most hardened of men. *Ven conmigo sin miedo,* she said, and into her arms I stumbled, beginning the peasant's exile from which I have yet to return.

The Walk (Early Morning, Pereira)

At 8 a.m., following the first Mass of the day, once the incense had clouded the church and obscured the sight of widows,

you celebrated independence from terror by walking around the fountain of the town square—gamines chasing each other

with split wood, or breathing from a paper bag, its contents relieving the torment of hunger in one-thousand fires. At the turn of every hour,

you took a workman's pride in the persistence of your heart, which had, in its ninety years, understood much grief and strain. And yet, Miguel,

victory would have to wait for yet another instant, for yet another year for peace to loosen its mask. Elsewhere, leaves broadcast their warning:

notes on disaster in color and texture, in light and water. As you turned the corner towards home's crucible, the men approached you, promising

not to slur body and memory: "We're not going to hurt you, old man —we only want your shoes." They lifted you, giving the appearance of

ceremony, by the elbows, whose skin must have felt as thin as parchment paper. "Forgive us, *abuelo*," one of them said, "but we are no longer afraid."

Now, in bare feet, you returned to those remaining steps, your daughters not knowing the reason for the delay in your arrival, wreaths of white roses

in miniature encircling their necks. Running eastward in the direction of the church's spire, they found you, shaken yet resolute. "Children," you sighed, like the cancelled throat of God, "they were only children, much like the ones your mother gave me, all those tired years ago."

Trust

In a room above a thousand
unborn choruses,

a mother gathers errant bath-
water with her blouse.

American Nocturne

I
Father was a terribly difficult man.

II
I've been asked to write about Father, to clear up some misunderstandings and ameliorate the harm caused over comments he made over the years—but I don't want to turn this discussion into an academic paper, an opportunity for gossip, or a case study in psychoanalytic theory. I simply want to note that Father, always Father—raised in the Church, only to later renounce God—was a man whose idea of affection was watching you walk across Queens Boulevard with cotton-and-bead-stuffed Teddy, while waving a tongue-red lollipop, teasingly, between the thumb and forefinger of his left hand.

III
Father had a love of violence, especially the controlled and sustained violence of boxing. On Saturday afternoons he watched bouts televised from Las Vegas and Atlantic City (or was it Monaco?) while holding a pair of longneck beers in both hands and, raising them to the sky, blared at the screen with the intensity of an infant suffering from her first experience with colic: "*You ain't a fighter if you can't protect the face—protect your fucking face!*" And from the threshold of the kitchen I stood in bare feet with what I imagine was an uncontestable hunger, awaiting the first opportunity to answer Father, to show him the face of the truly bloodied.

IV
I spent desperate years trying to please Father. I tried to make him see that I was his son, Son of Father, but he let it be known that he had little use for me, the last of his three children. I was, as he so delicately put it, a momentary mistake made permanent—like soldiers who went to Korea, only to return home with the devastation of mangled limbs or the clap—a mistake that arose out of a chance meeting with an ex-girlfriend, the edges of her pleated skirt framed in sweat and tympanic rage, in the parking lot of a local supermarket.

V

A man can do much less with what he is given—*far less.*

VI

After the first morning chimes of the wall-clock I found Father, sitting at the Formica table in the kitchenette, resting his head on his right forearm—thinner if more mottled than most—the other arm hanging languorously under the table; his breathing was labored, seemingly leaden, as if he had spent time learning the consequences of age by walking across hills, rivers, and chasms not previously marked by the misery of man. I wanted to spell out the individual letters of his name, to have him hear me—this little boy—speak as if for the first time, but my throat caught itself, strangled by a mist or fear smothering the body—

VII

From Father I learned how to sleep alone, as if revisiting time spent in the womb, in order to confront the anguished feeling that something, if not *someone*, had been irretrievably lost like lattice patterns, shattered, or a silver cross thrown by the night watchman from the docks into the passive ache of a waiting sea, a waiting sea.

VIII

In the extinguished hearth of a confessional Father once dreamt: A playing card turned over; a man consumed by solemnity; the leveling of the tide.

IX

After a particularly cruel encounter with M_____, Father called me into his room, sat me down on the fold-out bed, and offered a sheaf of papers on which he had written, in a turbulent scrawl akin to screaming, the lessons his own Father had failed to teach him. He then ground with violence the crescent-sun of his thumb's nail beneath each word, rendering each syllable, the scythe of slanted tones, a physical form. Every crease in the bleached pulp was a reflection of my own interminable terror: *You are your own sin.*

X

Father picked up the broadsheet, folded it carefully into quarters, and pointed to an article on page 25A. The article said that scientists in Europe had discovered a rare fungus known only to affect flightless birds, which might explain the recent string of avian deaths—*the colorful plumage settling on the lake was nothing if not suffocating*, was one particularly memorable line—in bodies of water from France to Estonia. Father bent his shoulders forward, cleared his throat, and asked in the tone of clerics and conspirators:

If you found a helpless bird on your walk, would you prod it with your tongue, give it a new name?

Call Me Father, Call Me Wanting

The maternity ward, on the third floor of the Saint Monica general hospital, is open for viewing to the public on those Wednesday evenings, Friday mornings, and during select hours when an accent of black hawks serves a remote echoing. A sign, off-white, in raised lettering (*the pressing of no tempest is to be translate*d) faces the nurses' station and instructs visitors to speak softly, lest the warped trill of their throats' tenor causes a stillbirth. (Today, there will be no wrappings in leather, gauze, or the remains of the lowered flags—those husks removed at blackened partings.) I visit the hall at least once a week, a clutch of white roses in the crook of my arm, hoping to engage the attending nurse in conversation:

Have they been crying?

*Their laments sound like the steady
crescendo of air sirens,*

so complete is their arrival.

*

On the reverse of a card embossed with his name in gold, given as an offering: *Eu sou possuído por ninguém*—I am owned by no one.

*

Dear Father,

It has been close to a year, closer, since your last message. And yet you persist as night tremors, your scythe's curve an implosion: lucid and enduring as imprints of canine-teeth on torsos, or a palm bearing an unspoken heaviness, and this—the filament that is our fractured narrative.

*

On the margins of the birth certificate, rooted like wolves' snow-bound coursings, I have written what had been kept in disguise, now a rising of dust across the face, through these rooms of recollection:

Call me your son,
   a vanishing of salt.

A Simpler Language

Another day arrives on the shoreline, and fishermen crawl northward for forgiveness, their hands a trial of bent wires.

*

On street corners, children speak of a simpler language, of cloth loosening from limbs, of breathing without struggle.

*

The cantor comforts his throat with tea and grace, summons a tenderness that will go unanswered: the boulevard opens like a current of swallows.

*

The road leading to the lighthouse is closed for the winter. Hired men stand guard, rifles in waiting, memory underfoot.

*

A pleading of dogs tightens around the elderly, shaping waves of dust and tones, the animals' haunches lacerated by dread.

*

They stand, in borrowed headscarves and with oiled faces (for the sake of protection), at the threshold of his bedroom: "The doll with flaxen hair was right," he says, "I already feel my belly beginning to harden."

*

While in the bath, a woman tends to her waiting breasts with caution, as if learning to walk for the first time.

The Ballad of the Pantera Negra

It has come to this, hija, she remembered. It has come down to this, she once heard her great-grandmother say, to the shame that consumes the lives of my children, my neighbors, this sickly body, but she could find no possible way to respond, to react in kind; there was no triggering of electrical pulses with which to set shoulders or fists in motion. There were no words to complement the range of calamities so eloquently detailed in the beaten, discolored diary once kept by the women in her family and passed down to succeeding generations, and whose origins lie in the manifests of slave ships bound for Barbadian ports from Bristol and Liverpool, from Lisboa to the scrum rising in Recife, from Catalonia to Cartagena's burned shoreline. So burned by the light of the golden cross were those sands, its peculiar strain later recorded onto leaves as the heat of locust swarms elevating in the fields. This was a heat so punishing, a heat so grave and resolute, that no man could ever fail to repeat the warning: the infernal wave covered them, ate them, took them away, out of the fear that sons & daughters would suffer the same indignity that had proven itself a stain on the Veracruz family— living within their cells, grafting onto layers of blood as history, their chained dogs reduced to shocks of marrow and gunpowder.

The dread-current stalked the pilgrim's length of migration, as though a *pantera negra* reflected in streams, those caravans moving in a silence so profound that even children were unable to interpret the diamond-pressure in their fingertips or photograph the swollen casks of their bellies, veined growths borne not of hunger, but of a much quieter desperation; in this she found no manner of speaking, and she tired of the thought of needing to speak, of needing to provide *ausilio* to her great-grandmother, a woman with enough relics in her chest to overwhelm cities and statues of soapstone overlooking harbors, but lacking the pleas to confirm the full extent of human frailty, the letters of each phrase loosening from each other as though a net, engorged with the day's benediction, cut loose from its owner by the tide and lost to the unrepentant sea. Absent now are the flags to describe the shame that has kept her people from marking their names on dirt roads with oiled hair and their afterbirths, absent are the words in memory's language to denote the disintegration, softer, of the present;

perpetually absent is the shiv with which to carve *jamás* onto her own tongue.

The Bachelor Takes Inventory of All that He Owns, Values

He removes from his suit vest, a gift from Mother Superior, a box of matches; one deck of playing cards, wasting between fingers, soiled with ashen water; and a timecard, punctured to resemble a pattern of streams, roots, or the outermost edge of an orchid, pale as infant memory. Elsewhere a Victrola swings a ragtime 78, the record's tonal sweep beaten once more into night, into that hollow.

Later, into a tape machine on the corner nightstand, he will record the details of his life (the manner in which he recognizes the absence of God): the click and thrum of pages turned against their will; curious numbers and phrases—repeated only by an aged few—seen in newsprint, identification cards, and storefront windows; knuckle tattoos on thieves, vanishing in blurred lines; and the flaring crown and cross of the local pawnshop.

As his lungs expand and contract with these moments, he is mindful to tap his foot percussively, a soldier's persistent rhythm, as though attempting to recall his brothers in earlier years, when as boys they would run screaming into the streets:

Please, do not let us be taken—

A Brief History of the 21st Century

Did you want to be left alone? Mail-order catalogs, magazine reply cards, three-lane highways form an anxious necessity. What is the diagnosis, electric charge? To drag your body across the plaza—*Virgen de Guadalupe, ayúdenos*—is the dignity of penitence. I have returned for my belongings. In the mountains, children listen to the screaming undertow of war. The men inform me that I am very much alive, if tethered to sleep. At her mother's breast, an infant answers to the tyranny of faith. As of this writing, there are no casualties. *What are you, if not a series of vespers, note by slurred note?* More information, redacted, will be revealed following the commercial break. Tell me that I am pretty; please tell me that I am *wanted*. Without further intervention, the chances of a full recovery have been calculated at twenty-seven percent. I have learned to reclaim our blood-borne history. Prior to interment, the body must be cleansed in a ritual bath. Is there another name for hunger, a taste for the sacraments?

Harbinger

We learned to shape metal
with our hands,

to be cut without knowing
the tenor for *damage*.

*

Her beaded dress
is the phrase

that reads displaced
beams from light

towers.

*

Circling birds (

this raw choking,
fogged   cursive).

*

Children continue to speak
into hands,

veined coves:

> The balloon hangs
>   like a bloated dwarf
> on the branches
>   of an evergreen.

*

The news is crib death
is that severance which resounds

with the familiarity of blood.

Dismissal & Reverence

The fruit of a stranger offers an uncomfortable weight against the body. *Never fall for the sight of your own words* is the phrase of the day. What cannot be consumed is the difference between dismissal and reverence. The sharpest points collect just beneath the jawbone (hence the loss of taste and sensation). No questions that need to be asked are ever printed in the record of disease. The complex of pregnant canopies, a lyrical divide. Another beat that crosses into itself; rest-notes on a graph for seasons. Winds that leave casual bruises and depressions: designs of a lesser order.

This is the distress of sleep without form.

Litany

Farewell, retreating corner of sheath & mask.
Farewell, sight as breath as open arrival.
Farewell, multitude of lotus streams.
Farewell, wires strung across the chest.
Farewell, full air of anima-song.
Farewell, cantata through emptying rooms.
Farewell, threads circling bones, hour-shell limbs.
Farewell, silk of reason, denied memory.
Farewell, white-veil manner, cloud-lightness.

Farewell, though you tire and long for speech.

Danny Rivera is a writer and teacher from Brooklyn, New York. He received an MFA in Creative Writing from the City College of New York and an M.Ed. from Brooklyn College. His poetry and literary criticism have appeared in *American Book Review, Epiphany, Washington Square Review, Dislocate, The Laurel Review, Midway, The Lincoln Review*, and other journals. For more information, visit www.dannyrivera.co.

Eternal gratitude is owed to the following people, without whose help, guidance, and support this project would not have been possible: Laura Modigliani, Lucía Modigliani Rivera, and the extended Modigliani family; Cristina, José Manuel, and Steve Rivera; The Gaitán Family; Gregory Crosby, Reagan Lothes, and Benny Parekkadan; and all of my teachers, especially: Dympna Joyce, Deborah Landau, Eve Grubin, Elaine Equi, David Groff, and Wayne Koestenbaum. Special thanks to Leah Maines, Christen Kincaid, and the staff at Finishing Line Press.

This project is written in honor of the Colombian people.

www.ingramcontent.com/pod-product-compliance
Lightning Source LLC
LaVergne TN
LVHW041559070426
835507LV00011B/1196